WORDS OF WISDOM

Daily Affirmations of Faith

REV RUN

 AMISTAD *An Imprint of* HarperCollins*Publishers*

HarperCollins books may be purchased for educational, business, or sales promotional use. For information, please write: Special Markets Department, HarperCollins Publishers, 10 East 53rd Street, New York, NY 10022.

FIRST EDITION

Designed by Laura Klynstra Blost

Printed on acid-free paper

Library of Congress Cataloging-in-Publication Data has been applied for.

ISBN 13: 978-0-06-114487-5
ISBN 10: 0-06-0114487-8

06   07   08   09   10   ❖/RRD   10   9   8   7   6   5   4   3   2   1

DEDICATION

For my wife, Justine,
and my five wonderful children,
Vanessa, Angela, JoJo, Diggy, and Russie

**I WOULD LIKE TO ACKNOWLEDGE
SOME SOURCES OF INSPIRATION:**

Reverend Ike, Mike Murdoch,
Bishop Bernard Jordan, the King James Bible,
John Cook's *The Book of Positive Quotations*

INTRODUCTION

While I grew up, I was Pentecostal. I am now a member of a church called Zoe Ministries. I attend services frequently, and have been doing so for many years. I became so devoted to the church that I studied and successfully became an ordained minister. The founder and head of the church, Bishop Jordan, inspires the members of the congregation and helps guide them through their daily routines. For example, he once told the congregation, "If you take shortcuts, you get cut short." Simple, but that got me thinking about the direction I was headed in my life. His words inspired me to do things that I thought were beyond my capabilities. I went through a dramatic weight loss, started exercising daily, and founded a sneaker company called Run Athletics. I was feeling so good about myself that I even went back into the recording studio to lay down new tracks. For my personal edification, I began scribbling down my own words of inspiration, often referring to and reflecting on books I was reading. Some of those sources were the writings of John C. Maxwell, Deepak Chopra, and, of course, Bishop Jordan. I also referred to some of the world's greatest thinkers and philosophers, such as Sophocles and Aristotle. But my main inspiration came from deep inside of me and the words and teachings of Jesus. I began to sit with the bishop, whom I looked to as my mentor, seeking advice and sharing my words and reflections with him. He told me that my words were becoming so inspirational that I should start reaching out and sharing them with others.

The first place I went with my daily Words of Wisdom was the radio station Hot 97 in New York City. Every morning, Ed Lover and Dr. Dre would record me reciting my daily words and then they would put it on the air. It instantly became a regular and popular segment of the highly rated morning radio show.

Then I discovered the two-way pager. It immediately became my tool of preference for delivering my Words of Wisdom. I began by sending them out, every morning, to my closest friends, family, and others in the entertainment industry who happened to be on my e-mail list. This list included, among others, my brother Russell Simmons; P. Diddy; Gayle King, editor at large for O magazine; and Kid Rock. By word of mouth, my list of recipients grew. It expanded to business leaders, sports figures, and entrepreneurs. There were politicians on Capitol Hill who would sit with their morning newspaper and a cup of coffee waiting for their morning e-mail. Soon recipients began to forward my daily words to their friends. One particular person was sending them out to more than four hundred of his clients and closest friends. The feedback I was receiving was beyond my wildest dreams. One Hollywood movie director on my list told me that he wouldn't shoot a single scene until he consulted my daily words.

In 2005, three events dramatically changed my life. My brother Russell formed RSMG, Russell Simmons Music Group, and released my first solo album, *Distortion.* I was touring various radio stations across the country, giving interviews and promoting the album with my manager. Listeners called in to talk to me about my career and ask me questions about my new album. Some of them asked me about my daily words and how they could get them. I was amazed that awareness of my daily words was so widespread. As I toured, new DJs and program directors asked to receive my words of wisdom. Instead of just one radio segment in New York City playing them, radio personalities from Maine to California would read them, live on the air, every morning.

As if that weren't enough, MTV gave my family our own weekly television show. I would shoot all day, and go to sleep at night, only to wake up to the same routine. My life was on a difficult and demanding schedule. But there was one thing I refused to change. I would still wake up every morning and send out my daily words. The only difference was that the world was witnessing me doing so. They were more surprised to see where I was doing it. I was being filmed every morning sending out my daily words, using my new Blackberry, from my bathtub. It was unanimously decided that the bathtub scene would become the signature piece of the show, closing out every episode. My life continued to change, my family continued to challenge and engage me, but the words of wisdom always maintained their importance.

It seemed that everyone was aware of my daily words and wanted to receive them. Coincidentally, that's when I was approached to write a book. So here it is, a book containing many of my Words of Wisdom, or WoW's as they are referred to now, for you to read, learn from, meditate on, and get inspired by.

GOD IS LOVE

WORDS
OF
WISDOM

You must learn how to give before you can receive. Just as in nature, when earth gives forth its bounty, it gives seeds for the next season. We must learn to plant seeds for our harvest of health, happiness, love, success, and prosperity.

Your subconscious mind accepts whatever ideas you feed it and those ideas turn into experiences. Feed your mind the right ideas and your mind will lead you to the ways and means of manifesting those good ideas in your life.

You will get where you are going a lot faster if you look like you're already there. So dress and think as if you are the right person for the job. Your positive self-belief will give others a positive impression.

Get excited about the fact that God is in you. There are no poor people, only people who are not aware of the riches of having God within. GO WITHIN OR DO WITHOUT!

Life is all about love and your relationships. I have never heard a dying person say, "Bring me my awards, my medals, or my diploma." When life is ending, what we want around us are the people we love. The greatest gift you can give someone is your time.

Whenever I feel like I am lacking something, the first thing I do is to give. If you need love, give love. If you need a hug, hug someone. If you need friends, be friendly. If you need money, give some service. The law of giving and receiving is well and alive.

When you are disappointed, frustrated, or full of sorrow, make a plan to work at something and begin the work immediately. The *action* of the work will help you to refocus and to regain your positive attitude.

What do you do when you feel like nothing is going your way? What do you do when you feel empty inside and there is no hope? What do you do when you pray and your prayers aren't answered? Songwriter Bebe Winans wrote, "After you've done all you can, YOU JUST STAND." Psalms 46:10 says, "Be still, and know that I am God."

Giving is good. Sharing is good. My aim in life is to give away 99 percent and live off 1 percent. I believe if I keep giving abundantly, I will reap enough to reach that aim. Life is all about service.

When you're frustrated with results, never focus on the problem. Always focus on the solution. When you focus on the problem, it gets bigger. Here's one of my mottos: DO YOUR BEST AND FORGET THE REST.

We all want new and better experiences in our lives. Here's the trick: If you want new things, you have to think new thoughts. If you want a different result, you must begin to think differently. It's not so much what you do as it is what you think. Better thinking = Better doing = Better life!

In order to manifest any type of concrete blessing, you must be humble. There is no room for arrogance in the spirit. Touch and love others. The great have always been kind. The great have always been lovers of humanity.

GOD IS LOVE

Have a winning week. Here's the trick: In order to impress anyone, you must first impress yourself. Make yourself look good, smell good, and feel good. When you are confident, people can feel it. When you impress yourself, others will be impressed as well.

⌒

The only thing separating man from his desire is giving. People sometimes look for things they didn't work for. Luke 6:38 says, "Give, and it shall be given unto you." Foolishness is a farmer looking for fruit where he didn't plant seeds.

always tell my children to smile. I say people might have more talent than you in a certain area, but you can be happier than all of them! Smiling is a skill. Happiness must be practiced. When you are smiling, the whole world smiles at you.

Socrates said, "The unexamined life is not worth living for man." Are you a giver or a taker in life? What matters is not the duration of your life but the donation of it; not how long you live but how you live. Examine your life today.

Anything worth having is worth waiting for. Behind almost every success story there is a story about struggle. The real fun is in *creating* the success, not *showing* people your success. Looking for approval from others is wasted energy! Have fun on the journey.

We are all getting up today looking to receive something. But I say unto you concerning life—look to give, not to get. Don't look for a blessing, look to *be* a blessing to someone. Giving comes before getting.

Is materialism your reality? Things will never make you happy. In fact, they could make you sad if you don't have a relationship with God. You can and should have things, but don't let things have you!

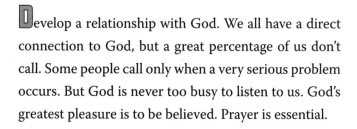

Develop a relationship with God. We all have a direct connection to God, but a great percentage of us don't call. Some people call only when a very serious problem occurs. But God is never too busy to listen to us. God's greatest pleasure is to be believed. Prayer is essential.

GOD IS LOVE

In Psalms 118:24, David writes, "This is the day that the LORD has made. We will rejoice and be glad in it!" Every day we must remember positive affirmations. The mind is like the body; if we feed it the wrong things, we become sick. Your thoughts are your prayers. Thinking right is praying right.

In many places, the Bible says that we must pray always. Praying always means that we must meditate on good things, joyful things, and happy things. Worry is the negative side of prayer. You must always keep your mind on Good. And who is Good? G O D.

Sometimes we have to step back and let God be God! Sometimes all you can do is *be*. Sometimes your doing is not helpful and you need to take a step back. Even God rested on the seventh day. In order to have peace, take some time to still the mind.

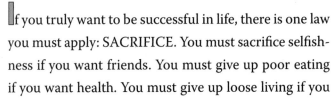

If you truly want to be successful in life, there is one law you must apply: SACRIFICE. You must sacrifice selfishness if you want friends. You must give up poor eating if you want health. You must give up loose living if you want a mate. Life is all about giving. In some instances, that means giving up something.

GOD IS LOVE

Walk in your God-given rights. Do not let sickness, disease, and poverty have a place in your life. It is not the truth of you. You are healthy, wealthy, and wise. You are exactly what God is! He created you in His image.

Learn to encourage people around you. Your children, your coworkers, and your family all need encouragement. If you tell a person that he or she is bad or dysfunctional, that's what you will get out of them. See and treat people in a way that you want them to act.

You cannot rely on what you see with your physical eyes. Imagination is creation. Here's the trick: You must hold the image of what you want in your mind until you can fully express it outwardly.

Your thoughts are things! In Philippians 4:8, the Bible says to keep an eye on your thoughts and to think on things that are true, honest, pure, and just, anything that is of good report. ". . . If there be any virtue, and if there be any praise, think on these things." Have a thinkful week.

You must learn to be a good listener. There is a reason why you have one mouth and two ears. You must listen twice as much as you talk.

People always ask me why I'm always happy. It's my faith in God. When a man knows that there is an invincible power that protects him and all that he loves, and brings him to every righteous desire of the heart, he relaxes all nervous tension and is happy and satisfied! It's not Don't Worry Be Happy, it's Don't Worry Have Faith in God.

In Galatians 6:9, the Bible tells us not to "be weary in well doing: for in due season we shall reap, if we faint not." That means don't become faint of heart when you know you are doing everything right and things are still going wrong! Harvest is near.

The most important thing I can tell you is to give. Giving is a universal law that cannot fail to bring results. What you put out must come back multiplied. Always remember, you only keep what you give away!

What is the cost of living? The only thing you must pay is attention. Focus and confront what is important. You cannot change what you don't confront. Things change when you change them.

❧

You are a salesperson and the person on sale is you. You are selling yourself every day. The question is: Do you love the product that is on display? Impress yourself first and then you will impress others. Root for yourself. Love yourself.

hoever said "It's not what you know, it's who you know" was only halfway right! It's both. In Isaiah 5:13, God allows his "people [to] go into captivity for lack of knowledge." We only prosper to the level of what we know, and lack of information kills. Get in the know.

I cannot express enough how important mentorship is. When you come to the end of your abilities and admit that you need help, life gets better.

GOD IS LOVE

Almost every time a blessing is about to arrive at your doorstep, adversity shows up to test you. Don't respond to the distraction! Stay focused, it's only a test!

If at first you don't succeed, try again. You will become depressed if you constantly look back at past failures. Falling off the horse is okay, but get up and try again. It's a new day.

ffirmations or positive thoughts are vital to your life-style. If you want to succeed, you must constantly feed your mind beneficial images of love and thankfulness and defeat all negative thoughts.

e thankful for every little thing. And be patient. Impatience delays your blessings and pushes you further away from your goals! The Bible clearly and so eloquently states in Zechariah 4:10, "For who hath despised the day of small things? For they shall rejoice. . . . Despise not small beginnings!"

I believe that before you start any new project, you should consult a professional who has successfully achieved that for which you are striving. Never work alone! Isolation is harmful.

Sometimes when life seems unfair and you feel that you are not advancing, consider this: Once upon a time there was a man complaining that he didn't have any shoes and then he ran into a man who had no feet. Don't worry, be thankful.

A real man or woman can admit to making a mistake. If you want to take credit for being right, you must say that you are sorry when you are wrong. If your children or those God entrusted into your care never hear you say "Sorry, I was wrong," you are not worthy to lead.

Life becomes a lot easier when you realize that life isn't easy, and was not designed to be. Who told you life was easy? Buddhists say the end of all suffering is acceptance. Smile and move on!

What do you think about you? How do you feel about you? Other people treat you like you treat yourself. You cannot really be mistreated unless somewhere in your life, somewhere in your mind, somehow you mistreat yourself. Be good to you!

Life is a stage and we are all actors in a play called life. We write our own script and revise it as we please. Who are you in this play? Are you sad, broke, busted, or disgusted? Or are you happy, wealthy, well dressed, and vibrant? It's up to you.

A wise man or woman will know when to work and when to rest. When you carry a burden or situation that you are not supposed to carry, it can destroy you. You can only handle so much. Let Go and Let God.

In order to succeed in life, you must take risks. The reason why people never experience better living is because they refuse to let go of the life they currently have. TAKE RISKS! Insanity is doing the same thing over and over and expecting new results.

GOD IS LOVE

You are always speaking your world of experience into existence. It's up to you to speak it as you wish it to be. Anything that you make clear in your mind, you are capable of doing. The more you become aware of the power of your mind, the power of your word, the more you will demonstrate it.

Decisiveness is powerful. The moment you make a decision, everything necessary for the fulfillment of your decision begins to happen. When you have a clear idea of what you want to be, what you want to do, what you want to have, you'll be able to create your own miracles.

We must always recognize that our innermost thoughts are prayers. Your inner conversation becomes your outward manifestation. Remember, thinking right is praying right!

Here is a funny thing about life: If you refuse to accept or give anything but the best, you very often receive the best! Stop looking for a blessing and be a blessing. Give the best. Get the best.

GOD IS LOVE

Start every day off in meditation or prayer. You cannot find peace or solutions with your mind racing or filled with anxiety. Go within yourself before going outside your house. Have a peaceful day.

Whatever you praise, you raise! Are you a thankful person? Are you going so fast that you can't see the blessing until it's too late? Look around at your loved ones and be *thankful*. Slow down and see the blessing!

Where is God? The Bible lets us know that God is within us. Jesus Christ didn't come so much to reveal himself but to reveal yourself. He performed miracles, but also in John 14:12, reminded us, "He that believeth on me, the works I do shall he do also and greater . . ." I believe you can fly!

Life meets you like you meet life. Set your day up every day with positive affirmations. You must make yourself happy. Being happy takes practice. I find that every time I say I'm thankful, I end up with more for which I am thankful.

GOD IS LOVE

What are you focused on? What are your goals? What are your desires? Our desires are far more motivating than our needs. Desire inspired the Wright brothers to fly. Desire motivated Thomas Edison to persist through ten thousand experiments before perfecting the lightbulb. FOCUS. Don't surrender to the distraction.

When I look back over my life I realize that I only feel great when I'm serving or giving in some capacity. Maybe that's why the Bible says it's *better* to give than to receive. Maybe that's why when some people give and someone says "Thank you," they say in return, "No. It was my pleasure."

Love must start with you. You cannot love or be loved correctly until you love yourself correctly. Your love life is the result of the way you love yourself. Your relationship with others is the result of the way you relate to yourself. If you want to love and be loved, you are the starting point.

What is a miracle? What is luck? I believe the harder I work, the luckier I get! I believe that our habits create our blessings.

GOD IS LOVE

Teamwork makes the dream work. Always remember, your network determines your net worth.

LIVE IN THE NOW! When I am anxious, it is because I am living in the future. When I am depressed, it is because I am living in the past. We crucify ourselves between two thieves: regret for yesterday and fear of tomorrow.

We are what we repeatedly do. You must despise where you are before you will ever be where you want to be. You simply set goals. You must have a goal to measure progress. Set one goal today, enjoy the process, and don't stop until you are done.

What is your lifestyle? Two of the basic ingredients that contribute to a person's lifestyle are routines and habits. You can yell, scream, cry, and pray about a routine you want to break, but if you can't change your habits, you can't bring about a better life. If you want to lose weight, I suggest a triple bypass: bypass bars, restaurants, and bakeries!

GOD IS LOVE

Stay encouraged. If you can find what you're excited about, you can find your money. If you can find what excites you, you can find your mentor. Many people are depressed because they have not found their calling. Many sell out for money or out of desperation. I tell people, do what you love and the money will follow.

You don't need to know everything. There is great wisdom in uncertainty. I would rather live in a world where my life is surrounded by mystery than live in a world so small that my mind could comprehend it. You don't know everything and you don't need to! Let go and let God. Remember, sometimes the blessing is in the mystery.

The world is full of people looking for spectacular happiness while they snub contentment. I have discovered over the years that riches are not from an abundance of worldly goods but from a contented mind.

No one is perfect. You might be a little scared, jealous, greedy, angry, but it's okay. Rather than deny or bury your feelings, you can open up to them. Cut yourself a little slack. Give yourself a break. No one is gonna bat 100 percent or even close to it. Get used to it. Every time you mess up this week, say these words: "I'm not okay, you're not okay, and that's okay!"

GOD IS LOVE

Treat every day as if it were your last. You never know when your time is up. I wonder about the people who die in car accidents on the way home. Did they tell their loved ones how much they love them? Do you hug your spouse or children enough? Cherish life! Cherish today!

How do you find your God-given talent and assignment? The answer is to find what you love. Here's how! If you could only earn one hundred dollars a week no matter what the job was, what would you pick? That's your assignment.

It's all you! Never point fingers at anyone, it's all your fault. The only person you can change is yourself. As you change, all the conditions around you will change! People will change! When you are undisturbed by a situation, it falls away of its own weight.

Have Faith. God's greatest pleasure is to be believed. His worst pain is your disbelief. How would you like to hear your children telling their friends, "Well, my mom and dad lie to me all the time. I just don't believe anything they say." You would be crushed. The same with God! READ SCRIPTURES. HAVE FAITH. BELIEVE.

Don't let life's ups and downs jerk you around! Do not worry or become stress-filled when you cannot change your circumstances. Let Go and Let God! Let this statement become your affirmation: I now cast my burden on God within and walk in freedom. HAVE A STRESS-FREE DAY.

I cannot stress the importance of prayer enough. You must have a connection to the infinite in order to have intuition or to be able to sense if you are on or off course. When you say, "Something told me I should have done such and such," that something is God. God is your intuition, God is your sense of knowing. Pray, Feel, Hear what God is saying!

Be kind to others. Take notice of the way you feel after you put someone down, notice that you feel worse than before the put-down. Here's a good code to live by: CHOOSE BEING KIND OVER BEING RIGHT. The compassionate part of you knows that it's impossible to feel better at the expense of someone else!

Time is money. Time is the currency of the earth! What you do with your time is crucial. People who spend time in the gym end up with great bodies. People who spend time with their spouses have great marriages. The healthy and wealthy aren't given twenty-six hours a day and the poor twenty-two; they just budget their time better.

GOD IS LOVE

What is your self-concept? To win in life you must first change the way you see yourself. What pictures do you currently have of yourself in your mind? Find projects you can excel and thrive in. The more you experience successes, the more the Polaroid picture inside of your head begins to change for the better.

Planning is so important to succeed! Here is a great thing to remember: If you fail to plan you plan to fail! Donald Trump also said something that stuck with me. "Failing is okay, but you should never be shocked when you fail." I believe that we all know when we didn't prepare for a task, so set yourself up to win.

Put a little gratitude in your attitude. Learn to be grateful. Never compare your blessings to another person's. I believe that if we become very thankful for small things, big things are right around the corner. GIVE THANKS TO THE LORD FOR HE IS WORTHY!

GOD IS LOVE

Money is great in that it provides you with options. If you have very little money, you have fewer choices. If you want to live close to your job and it's located in an expensive part of town, it might not be possible if you lack proper funds. If you want a car but can't afford one, you'll have to continue to rely on public transportation. Money is not everything, but freedom is, and if you want freedom you'll need money. Be diligent. Spend wisely.

Giving is a universal law that always brings results. Receiving is important also. The farmer plants his seeds and when harvesttime comes he must work and collect the fruits. There is a law of receiving that balances out giving. Giving is just receiving inside out!

Stay encouraged! A *Peanuts* strip once showed Charlie Brown with his head low and depressed. He said to Linus, "If you want to be depressed it's important to look depressed." He went on to explain that if you lift your head up and smile it would ruin everything and depression would fade away. Here's a trick: If you don't feel good, smile!

The Bible clearly states in Psalms 82:6 that "Ye are gods." So in essence YOU are God. Not the GOD, but a cup of God. God is like the ocean and you are a cup of God. Make sure that you keep pouring yourself back into the ocean! Here's the trick: Never look for God. JUST BE! God is within!

Stop complaining. Become aware of your blessings. Everything you need or want is already in your life—just waiting for your recognition of it. Anything unrecognized becomes uncelebrated. Anything uncelebrated becomes unrewarded. Anything unrewarded eventually exits your life. Recognize your blessings.

The Bible says in Philippians 4, "Be Anxious for nothing." When you are full of anxiety/fear, the very thing you are seeking runs from you. When you are in a relaxed state of mind, your confidence results in victory! You are at a disadvantage in any business deal or situation when you are anxious. Relax. Always remember to do your best and forget the rest.

In order to have authority, you must be under authority! As long as you know everything, you will never find a mentor. People who are successful always have mentors. Here's the trick: When in the company of a master, you know nothing! Shut up and learn. True riches come from operating with a peaceful, thankful heart.

GOD IS LOVE

Whenever you want to accomplish something very important, you must put it in the hands of smart, reliable people. Then make sure you double-check on them. I find that no one will love your project like you do. Always remember, people don't do what you expect, only what you inspect.

When you are the guru in your circle you're in the wrong circle! Your friends are your cheerleaders, your mentor is your coach. Your friends see what you do right. Your mentor sees what you do wrong. Your best friend ignores your weaknesses. Your mentor helps you address your weaknesses. Always remember, your mentor's correction is for your protection.

True peace and joy comes from a relationship with your maker. People search for happiness through successful, exciting jobs, money, relationships, food, sex, drugs, and so forth. Personally, I've tried them all, and so have countless others, but nothing can compare to the presence of GOD. Here's how you get there: The Bible says in James 4:8, "Draw nigh to God and he will draw nigh to you." Pray.

What you can tolerate, you cannot change! If you can tolerate those extra thirty pounds, you won't lose them. If you can tolerate an unhappy relationship, you will have one.

GOD IS LOVE

What is true freedom? True freedom is having a free mind! Imagine having a closed parachute when it needs to be open! Your mind is just like a parachute: When it's closed, you crash; when it's open, you're safe. Free your mind and the rest will follow.

You get paid according to the problems you solve, not the problems you cause. If you solve big problems, you get big paychecks. Want more money? Give better service.

Don't be afraid of the dark. Before anything worthwhile is acquired you must experience a dark period. Right before any great breakthrough, there is usually great pain (ask any woman who has given birth to a child). Darkness is not a bad thing! Isn't a darkroom necessary for any good picture to get developed? In Psalms 30:5, we learn, "Weeping may endure for a night, but joy cometh in the morning."

What is a dark night of the soul? Depression? Sadness? Let's look at life as if it were a musical symphony. Can we use dark sad notes as well as bright happy notes and make beautiful music? YES. Life is a roller coaster full of ups and downs. Enjoy the ride!

We as human beings have a power within us that strives toward self-betterment! But beware of striving only for self-aggrandizing power. Your talents are a gift from God for you to share with others. We are here to serve each other. No more, no less.

Get into the habit of winning. Winning is not a some-time thing. You don't win once in a while. You don't do things right once in a while. You aim to do them right all the time. Winning is a habit. Unfortunately, so is losing. Strive for perfection. It's a way of life.

GOD IS LOVE

Become obsessed with your assignment. The best way to disconnect from wrong people is to become obsessed with doing the right thing! When your obsession is to do the right thing, wrong people will find you unbearable. When I think back, I remember being extremely focused to the point of obsession while forming Run-DMC. Remember, you will succeed only when your assignment becomes an obsession! Stay focused.

TRUST THE PROCESS! Dreams happen when people stay dedicated to a process. Many people become excited about an idea and then quit because they lose their faith and become impatient! We don't know how a fetus's eyelashes, fingernails, and eyeballs grow inside of a woman's womb, but we still trust the process. Do your best and let God handle the rest!

What do you expect? Faith is expectancy. We hear people say, "The worst is yet to come." They are deliberately inviting the worst to come. We hear others say: "I expect a change for the better." Change your expectancies, and you change your conditions!

There are some precious gems we can find in failure! Never call your so-called failures stumbling blocks, but use them as stepping-stones. Every overnight success was birthed over many nights and much toil. The true secret to success is going from failure to failure without losing enthusiasm.

GOD IS LOVE

In Luke 14:11, the Bible says he who humbles himself will be exalted. Most people think that Scripture means that God honors those who are humble (head down, quiet, meek) before magically rewarding them! NO! That Scripture actually means that people with poor mind-sets have too much pride and don't ask for anything! A truly humble person has no problem asking for help and then they are exalted. Ask and it shall be given.

Of all the important things in your life, the one that matters most is your idea of God. Some people have created an angry, stingy God. In the book of Exodus, God instructed Moses to tell Pharaoh that I AM sent him! God is the Great I AM! God says I AM whatever you want me to be. You are the maker of your God. I don't know about you, but I have a happy, generous, loving, and kind God. Only think of God as Good.

Here's a new take on an old saying: SOMETHING HAS GOTTA GIVE! When things are going wrong, something has got to give, and that something is YOU. Life is thrown out of balance when any person withholds what belongs to the universe. People with problems are those who are out of balance with the universe. Give in order to restore balance in your affairs. Whether tithing, charity, or giving your time, remember, something has gotta give.

In the beginning God brought Adam every animal and told him to name them. After Adam named them, that was the name thereof! God brings man things and situations to see what he will name them. If something or someone lands on your plate that you dislike, you have the power to name it good or bad. Lemons or lemonade. Roadblock or stepping-stone.

GOD IS LOVE

Birds of a feather flock together. That is the law of attraction. The word "attract" means to draw. You are a magnetic field of mental influence. That about which you constantly think, you pull, draw, and attract toward you. What you attract depends upon that which you dwell upon in your thoughts, words, and actions.

Men only fail because they lose enthusiasm. Many people start with a clear vision, and then when things get blurry, they stop. Never share your dream with people who don't have similar dreams. Winners hang with winners, and losers hang with losers. I don't need a crystal ball to predict your future; all I have to do is look at the company you keep.

We all have dreams that we want to materialize. In Genesis, Joseph had a grand dream, and his brothers hated him for it. Rule number one is everyone will not celebrate your dream. When you have a big dream some of the people closest to you will discourage you. Joseph never doubted his dream and kept on dreaming and went from slave boy to Prime Minister. Never stop dreaming. Never!

Love is the most powerful principle you can work with! A noted psychiatrist has stated that the greatest human need is the need for love, and that none of us can survive without it. Love is the greatest power on earth. Here is a way to make love work for you. Affirm these words every day and watch the magic begin: *I love all people, and all people love me.* It will bring harmony.

There are definite rules that will bring happiness and joy to you, but you must follow the path of enlightenment. The first rule is contentment. The second rule is simplicity. The third and most important is thankfulness. People suffer because of desire. Once you become very thankful and count all your blessings you will be on your way to enlightenment! Be content . . . be thankful!

Positive thinking is very important. The best way to begin thinking positively is to talk to God constantly. Develop a relationship with God and nothing will be able to stop you. Stay in constant union with God. A very good book to read concerning positive thinking is *The Power of Positive Thinking* by Dr. Norman Vincent Peale.

Today we will talk about the process versus the prize. We must learn to enjoy the process! Do you enjoy the creative process of writing poetry, decorating, drawing, helping others build a company, entertaining, serving people with excellence? Never, never chase the prize, which is rewards, awards, or pats on the back. The process is the prize, so have fun while you are at it.

GOD IS LOVE

How do you receive answered prayer? The Bible says ask and you shall receive. And in asking, you must be definite with the infinite. Until a man selects a definite purpose in life he dissipates his energies and spreads his thoughts (prayers) over so many subjects and in so many different directions that they lead not to answered prayer but to indecision and weakness! Make up your mind.

In order to have peace, make money, or to stay healthy you must put mind over matter. Never let problems become your reality; you must always appraise your mind higher than the matters that seek to disturb your peace. It's all in the mind. The eyes behind the eyes! You must always imagine greatness and never let your circumstances rule. Always value mind over matter.

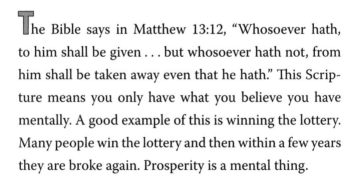

The Bible says in Matthew 13:12, "Whosoever hath, to him shall be given . . . but whosoever hath not, from him shall be taken away even that he hath." This Scripture means you only have what you believe you have mentally. A good example of this is winning the lottery. Many people win the lottery and then within a few years they are broke again. Prosperity is a mental thing.

GOD IS LOVE

Stop all negative thought! Think only about what you want, and never think about what you don't want. If there is something in your life that you do not want there, stop fighting it. Forget it! In 1 Thessalonians 5:22, the Bible says to shun the mere appearance of evil. Think positive thoughts all the time! Think happy thoughts, thankful and exciting thoughts! In case you did not know it, being happy is a choice!

The healthy and wealthy have self-discipline! To develop a lifestyle of discipline, one of your first tasks must be to challenge and eliminate any tendency to make excuses! Then stay focused on results. Never focus on the difficulty of the work instead of the results or rewards. If you do, you will develop self-pity instead of self-discipline.

We would all like to change some things in our lives: lose weight; acquire more money, leisure time, peace, and harmony; work toward more quality relationships; and so forth. But remember, what you can tolerate, you cannot change! You will never conquer what you refuse to hate. Anger is the birthplace for solutions and what you refuse to confront you cannot change.

Only 3 percent of the United States population has written a list of their dreams and goals. Maybe that's why 3 percent govern the other 97 percent. Three percent own as much real estate as the other 97 percent combined. And the same 3 percent possess as much wealth as the remaining 97 percent combined. Write down your goals!

There are many things that we want that are not good for us and God knows this. There are things that the Spirit protects us from for our own good, yet we still try to force it. There is a Divine design for everyone. Each day we must live according to the Divine plan or have unhappy reactions. A good affirmation to say is: If it's mine, I can't lose it—and if it isn't mine, I don't want it.

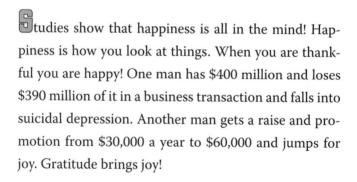

Studies show that happiness is all in the mind! Happiness is how you look at things. When you are thankful you are happy! One man has $400 million and loses $390 million of it in a business transaction and falls into suicidal depression. Another man gets a raise and promotion from $30,000 a year to $60,000 and jumps for joy. Gratitude brings joy!

GOD IS LOVE

The difference between success and failure is information. If you sincerely want to succeed in life I suggest two things, the acquisition of knowledge and determination. Study those who are successful and do what they do. It's very simple: The key is mentorship. If you can follow in the footsteps of winners you too can win!

Are things being held up in your life? Or are things flowing smoothly? Sometimes things around you do not flow because you are holding resentful thoughts or anger toward someone or something. Let it go and things will flow. Take a spiritual colonic and let life begin to flow for you. Let it go. Let it flow.

Focus, Focus, Focus! You will only have significant success with something that is an obsession. Success comes from having passion and having fun creating your objective!

Be happy! Happiness comes from contentment and gratitude! A great way to be happy is to train ourselves to be grateful for everything that has or has not come into our lives. Being content doesn't mean that you walk around letting anything fall upon you without efforts to create what you want. It's balancing between hard work and trusting in God's timing. Be patient! Father knows best.

GOD IS LOVE

If you want to change how you feel, you must change what you do and what you think about! What makes you happy? Writing music, performing comedy, traveling? Set yourself up to feel good. Plan ahead and adapt to changing circumstances. Life is like a play; if you don't like the script, tear it up and rewrite it.

What is a righteous man? A righteous man means one who is right with the universe, one who lives in accord with the Divine Will and the Divine Nature. Don't get it twisted. When you are operating in Divine Law, you will prosper. The Lord is the Law! The Law Thy God. God has everything in order. Nothing is chaotic. You will not and cannot break the Law because if you do THE LAW WILL BREAK YOU.

You often hear people say, "Something told me I shouldn't have done that" or "Something told me I should have stayed home." That something that speaks to you is God. Obey your intuition. You have a guiding instinct that helps you navigate on earth, but if you keep ignoring these instructions they show up less and less. Meditate every day and hear God.

Giving is the proof that you've conquered greed. I cannot express enough to you the power of giving. All throughout the Bible, in order to restore order in someone's life an offering is brought to priests and places of worship. Abraham was even going to sacrifice his beloved son in order to get God's approval. Giving is the only way to prove that you have faith. God is a giver. Have faith in Giving.

GOD IS LOVE

You wish to reap joy, happiness, health, harmony, and success. Can you be expected to keep your mind filled with such thoughts for yourself if it's not filled with similar thoughts for others? Of course not! The Scripture says love your enemies. You have no room in your mind for negative thoughts if you want positive results! Wish for everyone what you want for yourself.

I am extremely excited to tell you that you control your destiny with your imagination. The great Christian Yogi Paramhansa Yogananda once said that your imagination is God! Here's the trick: Picture what you want and keep seeing it until it appears. You must focus your vision every day and be very diligent in seeing it! In conclusion, when you believe you, I believe you!

Let's focus on how we can *be a blessing* instead of how we can get a blessing. How can we help our customers, boss? How can we serve? Let people leave you saying, "Wow, you are great at what you do!" Try to give more than you take from your job. Make others feel that you are so necessary. The real fun is seeing other people satisfied with your efforts.

Intense effort is the name of the game. Anything that is worth anything takes a brick-by-brick attitude. Persistence can and will overcome any resistance. Whatever you pay attention to will eventually pay attention to you. Whatever you neglect will begin to fall apart.

GOD IS LOVE

Start to see yourself excited about life. Learn to put exclamation points into your thinking and into your way of living. We must wake up every morning like a child! Each day, fill your mind with great energy and exciting expectations for the day. You are a winner! Remember your past victories and keep in mind that if you did it before you can do it again.

The key to being successful in life is overcoming obstacles! Are you a winner or a whiner? Winners anticipate problems, whiners only complain about them. Winners expect problems to show up, therefore they are not upset, they are set up! Stop complaining and become a winner not a whiner.

In Proverbs 23, the Bible says that "as a man thinketh in his heart, so is he." You must have correct self-awareness. You are always becoming that which you are conscious of being! Practice feeling good about yourself. Dress nicely. Fix up your environment, carry yourself with confidence, and never criticize yourself. Define yourself before someone else does.

GOD IS LOVE

ever become a slave to the conditions that you are in. In Romans 12:2, the Apostle Paul said, "Be not conformed to this world." In other words, never let what you see in front of you control your life. Life is like a movie: Pick a role, a set, your costars, even the extras. If you don't like your movie, call for a meeting and rewrite the whole damn thing.

The test of a leader is taking the vision from me to we! The next time you need the definition of team, remember this acronym: **T**ogether **E**veryone **A**chieves **M**ore. T. E. A. M. Every great dream needs a great team. Teamwork makes the dream work!

Become very intense, even obsessed, if you want big success. Take notice that very successful people are very intense in achieving goals. My man Will Smith says weak people make you weak! Russell Simmons would not miss a day of yoga for the president! Stay disciplined! Get focused!

GOD IS LOVE

When you are in constant memory of the goodness of God, more good appears! Be thankful and consider heaven like unto the stock exchange! The more you praise and thank God, the higher your stock goes. Praise Ye the Lord!

Diligence is a must if you want a blessing. The Bible says in Proverbs 12:24, "The hand of the diligent shall bear rule." Always keep in mind, leaders pursue the company and presence of diligent workers. Proverbs 22:29 says, "Seest thou a man diligent in his business? He shall stand before kings!" Perhaps your money or recognition problem is more of a hard work problem.

How do you feel today? Actually, it doesn't matter! Never let your feelings take charge over your day. Create your own feelings. Tell your feelings how to feel. Life is a movie. The cameras are rolling. Make sure you are *acting* like a happy, successful person!

Look at your personal life for places where you've let things slip. Sometimes we settle for pretty good when only excellent will do! You cannot do the minimum and expect maximum results.

GOD IS LOVE

Developing a prayer life should be a top priority in your life. **Beyond God you need no other guidance.** The energy and passion that you have is God's gift to you. That get-up-and-go that you have is God's energy! That great health you have is God's great health. Be thankful at all times and life gets better; what you notice and recognize becomes greater.

Slow down every day and pray. Be very thankful, and life won't seem so hard. When you are thankful you are never disappointed. When you are thankful you have no time to complain about what you don't have. Look at your health, family, children, and other overlooked blessings and begin to thank God! This is what our Creator loves.

Think of life as if it were a video game. You must all get to the next level with practice and a lighthearted approach. If you don't win today, put in another quarter tomorrow. Work hard, play hard. When you are easy on yourself life is hard on you, and when you are hard on yourself life is easy on you.

There is only one way to stop feeling hurt, forgotten, slighted, unloved, broke, broken. When you feel any of these symptoms, help someone else to feel better and take the focus off of yourself. Life brightens up when you help others. You cannot solve problems while look-ing at yourself. Say these words daily: It's so hard to see when the focus is on me.

GOD IS LOVE

Just like a play on Broadway needs an audience to stay in business, all negative situations need an audience in order to continue. Never pay attention to things you don't like. Don't worry. Negativity feeds on fear and starves on faith.

Find your passion and you will find your money and calling. What you love is a clue to what you will succeed at. Always remember that you must build your life around your obsession. You will only succeed with something that becomes your obsession. This week unclutter your life of things that don't excite you. Let go!

I believe that one of the essential keys to your success has everything to do with the mentor that you choose. You will never move beyond the people with whom you are connected. If you really want to grow in all areas of your life, find a worthy mentor.

If you really want to be successful in life you must understand that your belief is everything! If you can become fully persuaded in your mind concerning what you want and believe, your wish will be granted. Here's the trick: You cannot share your dreams with everyone. Remember, silence is golden. Don't talk about it. *Be* about it! God Bless.

GOD IS LOVE

Stop rushing through life. Your day should be savored, not gulped down. Live in the present. You see, today is really the only place you will ever exist. When you get to your future, you will rename it—today. If you do not know how to enjoy today, you probably will not enjoy many days in your future. The past is history, the future is a mystery. Live now!

Strike revenge from your mind-set. Never fight fire with fire. The master Jesus said, "Overcome evil with good." Love your enemies. In other words, kill them with kindness. Always remember the final result of the eye for an eye, tooth for a tooth theory is two one-eyed men with gaps in their teeth. In the end, good old common sense and logic always prevail.

GOD IS LOVE

I believe one of the most important keys to my success is being connected to the highly principled folks with whom I associate. I also believe that who I choose as friends, business associates, and mentors not only determines my successes but more important who I will become. The times I have compromised this wisdom have led to some of my greatest failures. Be careful who you associate with. It can make or break you.

The one who learns how to control his thinking learns how to control his destiny. Nothing can save us but ourselves. The individual who will learn how to consciously change his thinking process can remold his destiny. We are continuously being drawn into situations or circumstances, sometimes against our objective will, but seldom against our unconscious will. All outward forms of behavior are the automatic results of our inner mental pictures. Keep your mind on Good and God.

GOD IS LOVE

When we are tempted to worry or take care of some situations in life, we should pray the prayer of commitment. God intervenes in our situations when we commit to the Lord our children, our marriage, and our personal relationships. Cast all of your burdens on God and don't touch them. Take a deep breath. Let Go and let God!

Life cannot help but to bless those that do their very best all the time. Those who continuously work very hard and intensely are those who get the results. Whether in marriage, business, or household tasks such as keeping your lawn cut, if you don't stay on your job, weeds will grow. Where your attention goes, power flows!

What you respect will move toward you. What you don't respect will move away from you. It may be a dog, a person, or even money. For instance, do you treat your money with respect? Do you fold your cash neatly or do you crumble it up and put it in your pocket? Do you balance your books, or are you always bouncing checks? If you respect money, it will respect you.

Always remember, *feeling* gets the blessing! How you feel determines what you receive! If you feel like a winner, you are a winner. Learn to feel good about yourself. Say good things about yourself. Your inner conversation is a breeding ground for future actions. Solomon writes in Proverbs 4:23, "Keep thy heart with all diligence; for out of it are the issues of life."

believe that you and your family, group, or organization is as strong as your last act of unity. When there is unity, there is success!!! Run DMC was only successful because of love and unity. Any basketball team that wants to be successful must work together. Remember, pray together, stay together. Unity is the key.

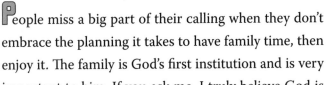

People miss a big part of their calling when they don't embrace the planning it takes to have family time, then enjoy it. The family is God's first institution and is very important to him. If you ask me, I truly believe God is a family man.

GOD IS LOVE

God has put something in you that others have not discovered! Never consult those who have not yet discovered what is special within you. Stop pursuing their conclusions. You know what you can do. Stop asking and start knowing! Go within or do without. God is on your side.

In *The Power of Positive Thinking*, Dr. Norman Vincent Peale writes that your relationship with Almighty God is imperative when it comes to thinking positive! Speaking with God throughout the day as a partner or friend is a great way to stay grounded and to become confident in your decisions. Believe in God, because God believes in You.

What is wisdom? In a multitude of verses, the Bible says wisdom is the principle thing. To make good decisions you must use wisdom. Your inner self has all the wisdom you need. Be still, meditate, think, and listen and you will find all of your answers. Relaxation and meditation are the key! You cannot find the right answers when you are speeding. Relax!

GOD IS LOVE

I totally believe that if we can't have order in our home, then having our business in order is almost impossible. When you get your home right, your money will follow. Remember, if you want to do better in fund-raising, then begin to raise your family.

ho are you? We must constantly remind ourselves that we are not the essence of other people's opinions. It takes tons of courage to be who you are and not let the rest of the world tell you what that is. No one knows how great you are until you show them.

he only way to be very blessed is to become very intense. The world can't help but to bless a diligent person! If you look at the lives of those who are very successful you will notice one similarity—they are diligent! Proverbs 12:24 clearly states that diligent people are blessed people.

Never let the size of your organization become your focus. Remember, small hinges swing big doors! At Disney a little mouse took the land by storm. First it was Disneyland, now people come from all over to Disney World. Bigger is not always better. Remember, the little mouse makes the elephant dance!

People are happy when everything is in balance. Remember, things will never bring you happiness! True joy comes from within not from without! Never depend on circumstances to make you happy. Circumstances change. God within you does not. True joy is found in His presence, not in His presents.

What are you looking at? What you see affects the decisions you make. Make your atmosphere worthy of your attention. If you like flowers around you, buy them! Do not wait and hope that someone will send them to you. Take the initiative. When you are set up . . . you won't be upset!

Remember, we are here on this earth to be stretched! When the pressure becomes unbearable don't let it get you down. God is on your side, and He won't put more on you than you can handle!

Who do you think you are? You are always becoming what you believe about yourself! The truth is, you are today what you believed about yourself yesterday. You will be tomorrow what you think about yourself right now. The Bible says in Proverbs 23:7, "As he thinketh in his heart, so is he." Go to a mirror and look at yourself and say: "I'm a winner."

The Bible says weeping may endure for a night but joy comes in the morning. The Lord sends new mercies daily! Sometimes the negative helps us appreciate the positive. . . . It takes negative and positive for electricity to work! It takes darkness and light to make up a day.

Keep going. Keep moving. We must continue to do the right thing day in and day out. Some seasons it will feel like nothing is moving for us. But remember, we must learn to trust the *process*, not our feelings. God sometimes uses seasons of silence to build character in us. Stay encouraged! Keep your eyes open! Look for the good in every day and you will find it.

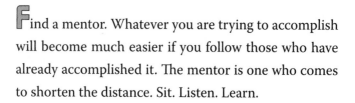

Find a mentor. Whatever you are trying to accomplish will become much easier if you follow those who have already accomplished it. The mentor is one who comes to shorten the distance. Sit. Listen. Learn.

GOD IS LOVE

The Lord is Good! I cannot express how Important it is to trust in him. All of your good luck and good fortune comes from him. The pressure that you feel is the hand of the Lord. Life is a series of good times, tests, and obstacles that you must balance. Don't forget to pray and count your blessings this week. And have fun while you are at it.

Energy is a precious resource! It is time to reexamine where and how you use your energy. Where can you put your effort so you can make changes that allow you to be more productive? What are your long-term goals? What about the people you love? Do you spend enough time with your family and children? Take time to see what's really important.

Where do you spend most of your time each week? Your answer will reveal what you love the most. Where your attention goes power flows! Great marriages require that you spend time together. Great businesses require that you take time to nurture them! Use your time wisely! Time is the currency of earth!

Look for the best in everyone! People around you are as valuable as you think they are. When you have a critical spirit toward your spouse, children, or helpers they become more of what you say they are! Learn to encourage others and they will perform better for you. Look for the best in everyone and you will find it.

GOD IS LOVE

Only by doing good for others can you attain your own good! Energy circulates in a constant give-and-take motion. The more you give the more you receive! By simply putting the goodness within you to work for others, it will flow back to you. The easiest way to get what you want is to give what you want to others.

God's voice is the only thing that is required for you to prosper! You might ask, "Well, how will I know God's voice?" The answer is: "Listen." The greatest decisions you have ever made came through contemplation. Your intuition is God's way of communicating with you. People always say, "Something told me not to do that!" Well, that something was God! As I like to say, "You must go within or do without!"

Who really has the power? I've seen people all over the world hunger for power. I've seen individuals who go crazy trying to prove their greatness! Chasing power is a sign of insecurity. What people are really chasing after is security. Remember this, security does not come from power. Security comes from self-love. Know who you are in God and who God is in You!

Did you know that your thoughts are capable of drawing people toward you or driving people away from you? Your attitude is sensed. You will never succeed in any business unless you really believe in that business. You must believe in the product you are promoting. Your doubts will surface and negatively affect others. You must believe yourself. Your thoughts are things.

Unclutter your life of things that do not excite you. When you are excited about a project others can feel that energy. Each morning when you wake up, begin to think about things that excite you! Get excited. . . . Let's go!

Do you have a guilt complex? Psychiatrists call man's failure to forgive himself a guilt complex. Some people have the habit of persecuting themselves and saying, "Oh, why did I do this!? Oh, why did I do that!?" When you beat yourself up you're sure to lose in this game called life. Forgive yourself. God loves you.

GOD IS LOVE

Focus! Focus! Focus! We must focus on every area that we want to be successful in. Your care and personal touch is the most important element in any business or relationship that you want to see flourish. The Bible speaks on constant maintenance in the book of Proverbs. Remember, you never get what you expect, you only get what you inspect!

Do you feel the need to rule? Do you strive to conquer others? A true leader knows he must rule only himself. To be a leader, you must first cast away your need for power and control over others. Many people yearn for power just to validate themselves. A true leader finds his unique talent for leadership is in service to his fellow man.

Enjoy the present! Are you waiting for that special occasion? If you're not happy right now, then it doesn't matter what's in your future—you could even win a free trip to Hawaii, yet once you get there you'll be waiting for the next high. The truth is, the only good time you will ever have is right now. Not when you get that new car and not when you get that new house. If you enjoy now, you'll have a much better time later!

The only way to really receive anything is to relax! Your manifesting has everything to do with knowing who you are and not feeling needy. You start with intention but you must detach from the results. Attachment is fear. Go for what you want, but you must relax and leave anxiety behind. Don't worry, be happy.

If you really want to succeed in life, intense effort is needed. You must constantly stay on your J-O-B. Anything you'll ever achieve will come from hard work and dedication! Here are two more success secrets for your journey: Find a goal that you enjoy and stick with it. Check your goals constantly and make sure you are still excited.

Do you want a prophecy of your future? Do you want to know where you're headed? Look at your friends and those closest to you and that is a prophecy of your future. Who you are around will show you what you are becoming. Birds of a feather flock together. If you want to change, change company!

Find out exactly what you love to do and stick with it. That's your calling and your path to money. This week remove the clutter from your life and focus on your love and strengths! You have a uniqueness that only you can express. Get focused!

You will never convince anyone about your projects or goals until you fully convince yourself. Do not present yourself or your project to those in positions of authority until you are convinced that it is foolproof! Become fully confident about who you say you are and how great your project is, and others will agree. People see you as you see yourself.

The saddest tragedy of life is a heart that has not caught fire. The most incredible thing that can happen to a dream is a specific plan of action. It births self-confidence! The four kinds of people who always fail are the undecided, the unlearned, the unfocused, and the unexcited. Stay enthusiastic, focused, and aggressively happy!

Take your time today! You cannot hear God's instructions while your mouth and mind are speeding. Take time to notice the small things. You can really enjoy life and accomplish more if you handle your day in peace. Take time to smell the flowers, listen to children, talk to a neighbor in need. Chill! Most of our mistakes are made when we are speeding.

GOD IS LOVE

We must give every heavy burden that we have to the Most High. When you come to a place when you cannot figure out which way to go, give it to God and relax. God loves it when you depend on him. This advice is not a cop-out for you not to take control of your life. But remember, it takes a whole lot of faith and trust to relax when you have a problem.

The only people who make it in life are those who take risks! In order to get the best fruit you must go out on a limb. The ballplayer who takes that last three-point shot from half court with three seconds on the clock gets the cover of the newspaper and MVP! If you are afraid, you won't get paid. In the hood they make it clear! Scared money don't get no money. Be daring.

Effortless living is never and will never be effective! Many people believe that we are working hard so we can relax when we retire. The truth is, the only place of true rest is the grave. We were created for involvement, participation, and struggle. We are not supposed to struggle with everything, but we are not supposed to give in easily either! Keep on keeping on.

What are you saying in your heart all day? Are you speaking well of yourself? Are you proud of yourself? Do you forgive yourself when you go astray? Do you love yourself? Look in the mirror and say to yourself: I AM Great. I Love Me. Your inward conversations determine your outward deliverance! You will be delivered from problems, but you must first deliver yourself.

Everything that happens in your world is a result of the state of your mind. When you get your mind and heart in order, this causes everything in your experience to get in order and stay in order. In Proverbs 23:7, the Bible says that as a man thinks, so he is. When you are at peace with yourself, everyone is at peace with you!

When you pray, always give thanks. Never tell God that there is a problem. Instead, thank God that the solution is on the way. Thank God for what you have, and that more will be added. Giving thanks and praise is what God likes. Don't tell God how big your problem is, only tell your problem how big your God is.

Multitudes of people have failed to live for the present. They have spent their lives reaching for the future. What they have had within their grasp today they have missed entirely because only the future has intrigued them. And before they knew it, future became the past. Have a great now!

The difference between the poor and the rich is that the rich invest their money and spend what's left, while the poor spend their money and invest what's left! Most Americans are busy buying things they don't want with money they don't have to impress people they don't like! Give wisely. Invest wisely.

Between 1970 and 1999 the average American family has received a 16 percent raise in income. We are better paid, better fed, and better educated. Yet the divorce rate has doubled, teen suicide has tripled, and depression has soared! Modern research has confirmed what one Roman philosopher said two thousand years ago, "Money has yet to make anyone rich!"

If you can think about your past problems, then you can think about future victories! Stop replaying your past hurts and pain. Thinking about past injustices can sometimes become more damaging than the experience itself. Use your imagination to see your wonderful future but never dwell on past failures.

Are you a good listener? The best way to show someone you love them is to listen to them. Have you truly heard your spouse or children? I'm a firm believer that if you listen to the whispers, you won't have to hear the screams.

What are you putting up with? Your silence about situations that you don't like is your vote for those problems to continue! You are worth only what you think you're worth. Remember, people treat you like you treat yourself. What you walk away from determines what you walk into.

Favor is when someone has a desire to solve a problem for you. Follow the path of favor wherever it is happening in your life today. Who feels kindly toward your life? Who has discerned your worth? Who has been the most used by God in your financial life in the last twelve months? God is presently using them for this season. Stop evaluating their flaws, stop building walls of distrust. Follow the path of favor and stop complaining.

Are you exhausted? Tired? Fed up? Have you tried everything to solve a certain problem and nothing seems to work? Here's the secret: Pray! Let Go and Let God! Standing still is action in God's economy. It is not irresponsible to enjoy life while admitting that we don't know what to do.

Why is the word *familiar* so close to the word *family*? Here's a clue! Do you know your children's teachers? Are you familiar with the kids they are hanging with? Get to know the people you live with and those who are important to their lives.

Timing is everything. It's good to have a big beautiful coat, hat, and gloves, but not in the summer! The Bible speaks about seasons and knowing how to number your days! If you are always late for work or appointments it sends a definite signal. Remember, tardiness is silent rebellion! Be on time.

GOD IS LOVE

Knowledge is power. So the question is, what do you know? Someone once said, "What we don't know won't hurt us." I believe that what we don't know can kill us. If you're in deep water you better know how to swim! The Scriptures say we perish for a lack of knowledge. Remember, never stop learning. Your knowledge is power.

Life isn't as hard as it seems. Here are some keys to unlock your success. Successful people shorten the distance for you. Become fascinated with them. Follow, pursue, and study the path of those who have what you desire. If you have the combination to the lock it doesn't matter who you are, it will open!

Today let's concentrate on being happy. Live life like a child! If you can capture the spirit of a child, life becomes much easier. Never let life's pressures bring you down! This is the day that the Lord has made—we will rejoice and be glad in it!

Become a giver. Life gives to the giver and takes from the taker. The Bible says in Galatians 6:7, "Whatsoever a man soweth, that shall he also reap!" If you want friends, be friendly! If you want love, give love. Stop focusing on yourself. The Law is in place. When you help others, life constantly sends help to you!

God wants to know one thing: What type of BS, or Belief System, are you on? How many people want to please God? Here's the key: Without faith it is impossible to please him! First things first. You must believe that God *is.* God's greatest pain is to be doubted, and His greatest pleasure is to be believed. Your belief system is everything to God.

The daily habit of picturing yourself as a winner filled with great meaning and purpose brings that picture into reality. Resolve that you will never have anything to do with inferiority in your thoughts or actions; that whatever you do shall bear the stamp of excellence.

Your attitude—not your achievements—gives you happiness. Fame and fortune are fleeting. The satisfaction that comes from achievement is momentary. Seek to be inspired. Develop a great attitude. The thoughts in your mind will always be more important than the things in your life!

Believe in God and have faith. We all have a lot of faith. Think about it. You go to a doctor whose name you cannot pronounce. He gives you a prescription you cannot read. You take it to a pharmacist you have never seen. He gives you a medicine you do not understand and yet you take it! Do me one favor. Now try praying to and trusting in God!

GOD IS LOVE

Many people allow their desires and longings to fade out. You must keep the fire burning every day! Reject all thought of enemies, all discouraging moods—anything that would even suggest failure or unhappiness. When the mind has formed the habit of holding cheerful, happy, prosperous pictures, it will not be easy to form the opposite habit! Stay happy! Stay inspired!

We must learn to take 100 percent of the blame for everything in our lives . . . EVERYTHING! This is not easy. In fact, most of us have been conditioned to blame something outside of ourselves! We blame parents, bosses, friends, or even the weather. Today, begin to take responsibility for all of your problems. Take matters into your own hands. That's a truly successful person!

Stay creative and have fun. . . . Remember to never ever take yourself too seriously. To lead a big company means never taking yourself too seriously, and reminding yourself constantly that yesterday's press clippings often wrap today's fish!

Make your family your friends. My wife and children are my best friends. I believe what Aristotle once said: "Without friends, no one could choose to live, though he had all other goods."

GOD IS LOVE

The way to be blessed in life is for you to be a blessing! You need to ask yourself two questions, "Whom am I blessing?" and "Whose quality of life am I helping to increase?" If you cannot find anyone whom you are increasing in life, then that explains why you are not increasing in life. Life gives to the giver and takes from the taker!

Make a decision to do the right thing continuously. Remember, if you take shortcuts, you get cut short!

Happiness is a decision you make, not an emotion you feel! You don't have to wait for everything to be perfectly straightened out in your family or with your business to experience happiness. If you are dieting, don't expect happiness to come when you've lost weight, be happy during the process. Don't let circumstances steal your happiness! Be happy now, it's a choice.

You cannot heal what you're unwilling to confront. Learn to develop an appreciation for truth. People tend to exaggerate their successes and minimize their failures and deficiencies. Face up to your truth. If you have money problems, weight problems, or marital problems, admit it and begin to work on it. Winston Churchill once said, "Men occasionally stumble over the truth, but most pick themselves up and hurry off as if nothing happened." Don't ignore your problems, develop a plan and work on them.

GOD IS LOVE

People often ask for things that they are not prepared for. God will not release your blessings until you are ready! Imagine getting five hundred gallons of water thrown at you as you stand there with an eight-ounce cup. You would get pretty wet! Many people want a Rolls-Royce right this moment, but they have only a Honda consciousness! Turn your oven on, lay out your best china, and the groceries will appear.

Turn your inner critic into an inner coach. Whenever you hear your inner voice judging you, simply reply, "Thank you for caring." Next, find out why you're beating yourself up and then respond with a plan to fix it. Remember, never say bad things about yourself without turning the critique around and using it to motivate yourself.

Find things to be thankful for. The perfect time to be thankful is when major problems arise! The Master, Jesus, never panicked when there was a shortage; he would simply lift up the problem and thank God that it was already done! Jesus only saw abundance. Be thankful. What you see is what you get.

GOD IS LOVE

Stay humble! Many times people think they know everything just to find out that they know nothing. Never act so smart that you end up feeling dumb. The Bible says that you can learn from an ant. Remember, the answers you're looking for are usually right in your face. Slow down, you've probably zoomed right past your blessing!

What is your financial psychology? Your attitude toward money will draw money to you or repel money from you! I hear people say all the time, "Well, money isn't everything." Never say what money *isn't*! Don't ever give money the idea that it doesn't matter to you. Never. Anything or anyone that doesn't feel that you have love and respect for them will run from you. God Bless!

Nothing is impossible with God! Here is a great principle that works if you dare to believe: *When you open yourself up to possibility thinking, you open yourself up to many other possibilities!* Most people don't think big, and that's why they do not prosper. Big thinking gets big results!

The law of change is great. You must refuse to settle down in a rut. If you don't give yourself a swift kick in the butt, someone else will. Remember to switch it up from time to time. Change your residence, diet, or job. Change is growth. Change is living. The law of change really works, it's real, and it will change your life!

You attract the things to which you give a great deal of thought and feeling. If you give much thought to injustice, you attract unjust experiences. Think and feel prosperous and happy. If you really want to be blessed, always remember your dominant thoughts and feelings capture those blessings!

All great blessings come from being at peace. When the day is over, go to sleep. Never sit up worrying about tomorrow. Work hard and let God do the rest. I always say these words at night, "I can sleep tonight because God is awake!" Relax. Rest easy.

You don't become rich until you understand service.

I firmly believe that our purpose in life is to make a difference in the lives of those around us. Make a mental and emotional commitment to look out for the interests of others. Always remember to be kind to others. Serve with a smile. Remember, people with humility don't think less of themselves; they just think of themselves less!

GOD IS LOVE

You cannot remedy anything by fighting or condemning it. Other people can't bring you down if you're operating on a higher energy level. Never respond to hate with hate. If you feel that those around you are bringing you down, it's because you're joining them in their low energy. Stay on a high note!

Let go of your need to have more. The mantra of ego is more . . . more . . . more. It's never satisfied. No matter how much you achieve or acquire, your ego will insist it's not enough. You'll find yourself in a perpetual state of striving without accepting the possibility of ever arriving. Yet in reality, you've already arrived, and how you choose to use this present moment of your life is your choice. Ironically, when you stop needing more, more of what you desire seems to arrive in your life. Enjoy, smile, breathe, and relax.

GOD IS LOVE

The one reason that my group Run-DMC was on point was practice. My motto is: If I miss a day of practice, I know it. If I miss two days, my manager knows it. If I miss three days, my audience knows it. Practice, practice, practice!

Many people feel that there is not enough room in their industry for them to be successful. Remember these words: Go that extra mile. There is always more room. Do more than you're asked, and you'll find it. The office is always empty at night!

Learn how to say NO! The key to getting what you want is rejecting what you don't want. Life is like a buffet. Take what you like and leave behind that which doesn't fit your greatest wish. Remember this quote: "What you walk away from determines what you walk into." Choose wisely.

How do you feel today? Here's a good answer to that question. . . . How I feel is never the point. We must constantly and consistently tell our feelings how to feel. Cheer yourself up . . . every day, all day. Always remember: The power is in your hands!

GOD IS LOVE

If you want to be happy, set goals that command your thoughts, liberate your energy, and inspire your hopes! Most people are doing things that don't inspire them; therefore, they are constantly waiting for weekends or vacations. Get to a place where when you have a day off, it almost feels like a distraction . . . That's when you know you're inspired.

Who's the genius who said "Don't put all your eggs in one basket!" I believe that you *must* find a definite aim and stick with it through thick and thin. When you pass on, they should be able to sum your name up in one word. If I say Jordan, you say basketball. Tiger, golf. Ali, boxing. If you focus hard enough on one great thing, you've done your job. Focus, focus, focus!

ost wealthy people have a core product. Determine your core product. If I say Trump, you say real estate. Bill Gates, software. Don't let people clutter your life with options or get-rich-quick schemes. What excites you? What do you love to learn about? Determine your core product and have fun with it.

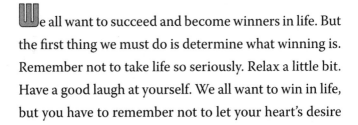

e all want to succeed and become winners in life. But the first thing we must do is determine what winning is. Remember not to take life so seriously. Relax a little bit. Have a good laugh at yourself. We all want to win in life, but you have to remember not to let your heart's desire become a heart disease. Loosen up a bit. Have fun.

GOD IS LOVE

We cannot change anything unless we accept it. Acceptance is not submission, it's acknowledgment of the facts of a situation, then deciding what we're going to do about it. Remember this, life's not easy. If you have a job without aggravations, you don't have a job.

There is a sense of accomplishment that cannot be denied when you do the right thing! There is also a sense of failure that eats away at your self-esteem when you don't live up to your potential. Self-image is extremely important. Work on your self-image daily. Look at yourself daily. Check the scorecard. How you see yourself is critical to your success.

You don't have to be terrorized by other people's expectations of you. YOU CAN SAY NO! Why do we find it so hard to say no to everyone's request? Highly successful people say no all the time. In fact, they view the decision to say no as equally important as the decision to say yes. When people call with another project for you to be involved in, you can say, "It's a very worthy cause, but I've overcommitted myself outside of my home, so even though I support what you're doing, I've got other commitments concerning family this week." Few people can get angry at you for making and standing by a higher commitment. In fact, they'll respect you for your clarity and your strength. Just say NO!

GOD IS LOVE

Never let how you feel dictate your mood. Train your feelings and they will obey you! Happiness takes practice!

Be kind, smile, shake hands, slow down, give love. . . . Simplicity is the ultimate sophistication!

Stay motivated! As long as I have a desire, I have a reason for living. Satisfaction is death. We must find a great reason to wake up every morning! Always remember, winning isn't everything. *Wanting to win is!*

Stay focused on your core genius. What excites you? What do you love to do? That's probably your core genius. Successful people put their core genius first! They focus on it and delegate everything else to other people on their team. When your money is acting funny, it means that you're not properly sharing your gift with the world. Work your gift. Get in where you fit in!

The greater the rejection, the greater the blessing. Don't worry about being different. Everything big that I've ever done was laughed at. Initially, mixing rock with rap, mixing a Rev collar with hat . . . dare to be different! Remember: "Any coward can fight a battle when he's sure of winning!" "The demand for certainty is a sign of weakness!"

Who are you? How do you define yourself? You must constantly define yourself! If you don't, others will! You are not other people's opinion. See yourself as you would like to be! Look at yourself in the mirror and say, "I am successful. I am a winner." Define yourself today!

People who have lots of money focus on getting lots of money, period! You get what you focus on. Maybe money is not your thing. Maybe it's not your top priority. That's fine. But if it is, then you must write down your financial goals and pursue them. Money management is a must. Work on your money daily! You can't heal what you refuse to confront. Have a healthy, wealthy day!

It is only as we take the attitude of stillness, of listening, of awareness that supply begins to pour out from within. So it becomes a matter of relaxing and letting supply catch up with us, instead of relying on people or things on the outside of us!

The Bible says "Be of good courage" many, many times for a reason. I believe God said this so many times because courage is a key to success. Confidence is a must. Move far, far away from fear. Fear is a thief! The acronym for fear is **F**alse **E**vidence **A**ppearing **R**eal!

You are a winner. Never give up. When you continue to move forward, day in and day out, you cannot lose! Even if they just ask you about a ball game that you lost, tell 'em, "I never really lost, I just ran out of time!"

Giving is a universal law. Always, always, always look for an opportunity to give. What do you need more of? More love? More hugs? More compliments? Then give the very thing you need away! Do you need money? Give what you have and watch it multiply. If you don't have any money, give through service. Just give!

GOD IS LOVE

First things first! Remember to do the things that produce the highest return first. If money is the priority for you, pursue financial stability first. If weight loss is something that will boost your self-esteem and solve health issues, exercise and eat right first. Ask yourself this one question daily! What are my priorities? What brings the greatest returns?

Get your shine on! When you shine, you give others the permission to shine. Never turn your shine off because you feel sorry for others. Don't believe that when you fall back, it makes others feel better. Inspire the world. When you shine, you light everyone's path.

What do you expect? Expectancy is a must when it comes to manifestation. The problem with most people and their prayer life is that they pray for one thing and expect another! The Bible says that when you pray, believe that you already received your objective. Remember, you don't get what you want; you get only what you expect.

Are you flirting with your goals or are you committed? If you are committed, remember this: Anytime you make a commitment to something, it will be tested. When you want to accomplish something, people will try to distract you. They will challenge you. They may even try to get you to compromise your values. If you desire to please yourself by following through on your commitments, there will be times when you will have to stand alone. Finally, the question still remains . . . are you flirting or are you committed?

Are you worrying? If so, stop, be fearless, and confront the facts. The next time you have worries, remember to ask yourself this: "What is the worst thing that could happen?" Finally, accept that whatever it is, it can't be that bad. Acceptance is the end of all suffering. Have a worry-free day.

GOD IS LOVE

Try something new! Many of us do the same things, day after day, for most of our adult lives. We go to the same places, hold the same opinions, and get upset over the same things. I'm not talking about trying a new job or career, although that may be a good idea, too. Instead, I'm talking about small inner changes that you can make on a day-to-day, moment-to-moment basis. Just once, try something different. If you're okay with the changes, which I suspect you will be, you might be inspired to try some other changes!

Let's talk about a sensitive subject: money. Let's look at money as a sophisticated lady. Money doesn't hang out with just anyone. Money has class, and if she feels disrespected she puts her nose up in the air and leaves the unsophisticated still wanting! Money is not a cheap trick, so if you use her unwisely she shows up less and less.

What's on your mind? The things that you are paying the most attention to expand! If your mind is constantly on eating, your stomach expands. If you are all about getting money, then your wallet expands. If you are attentive to your family, then you will have a happy family! Are you really focused on your career? Remember this: Where your attention goes, power flows!

GOD IS LOVE

Who is your real enemy? Your real enemy is ignorance. Get knowledge, learn and find out! Who made up that lie, "It's not what you know, it's who you know." Remember this: Life is a test and just because you know someone with the answers doesn't mean you will pass. Learn, study, find out. What you know determines how you flow. In the land of the blind, the man with one eye is king!

Passion is the number one quality for greatness. Passion is the energy to seek. Passion is the motivation to pursue. One of the things that I'm most thankful for in my life is my desire for winning. So many people lack passion. I have a volcano of craving for winning, to inspire others, for teaching, for rapping, for acting, for business. I thank God every day for my passion! Never, I repeat, never lose your passion for life. It's the quality that inspires researchers to find new cures and composers to write new music. Have a day full of passion!

What is your plan? Most people say they have plans for a great life. But remember this: A plan not executed is not a plan. A strategy not acted upon is not a strategy. I know what you *intend* to do, but intentions will not create a future. We must take action to create and design our lives. Get creative and take action today.

Who is the dominant voice in your life? From whom are you taking instructions? If you're only listening to yourself, then you are limited! Who you listen to determines what you do. You do not succeed because you have brains. You succeed because of what is in your brain. Information and education are the keys to success. Get informed!

Experience the satisfaction of unselfish thinking! The best relationships and partnerships are win-win. As you go into any relationship, think about how you can invest in the other person so that it becomes a win-win situation. Here's how relationships most often play out: If I win and you lose, I win only once. If you win and I lose, you only win once. If we both win, we win many times over. If we both lose, good-bye partnership! Stay focused on being your best self when relating to others.

Be happy and thankful. Seeds of discouragement will not grow in a thankful heart. Be ambitious, but remember that your true joy will come from the simple things. Benjamin Franklin once said, "Ambition has its disappointments to sour us, but never the good fortune to satisfy us."

Do you plan ahead? Are you strategic? Many people hope for a better future, but hope is not a strategy! Preacher Billy Graham is thought to be a very blessed and spiritual man because of his big turnouts in various cities. He is a blessed man, indeed. But the main reason he has big turnouts is because he sends out a team of people months before every appearance. Graham is an excellent strategist. We should all have great hopes, but hope is not a strategy. Planning is!

Be persistent. A number of years ago, Richard Bach wrote a ten-thousand-word story about a soaring seagull. It was turned down by eighteen publishers. Finally, it was published in 1970. Within five years, *Jonathan Livingston Seagull* had sold more than seven million copies in the United States alone. Seven million copies after eighteen rejections! The opinion of others has nothing to do with your success. Their rejection can only hurt your feelings, not your future. Stay excited about your vision!

GOD IS LOVE

We must learn to rest. Most religions call it their Sabbath. Many people in their ignorance get so focused on goals that they forget to rest. Take time to be still. In order to live a full life we must create a balance or we will miss life.

The formula for complete happiness is to be very busy. The only way to avoid being miserable is not to have enough leisure time to wonder whether you are happy or not. Here's the trick: We must devote ourselves to the strict and unsparing performance of duty, then happiness comes of itself.

Never try to be Mr. or Ms. Know-it-all. The greatest wisdom often exists in ignorance. The young do not know enough to be prudent and therefore they attempt the impossible and achieve it generation after generation.

Your ability to remain committed, no matter how hard it may seem, is the key to your breakthrough. If I were to question some of the last projects that you started, and they could speak, would they speak highly of you? Are they collecting dust in the corner, busted and disgusted? Finish what you start!

GOD IS LOVE

How you treat yourself determines how others will treat you. I know a young man who dresses nicely, eats healthfully, and treats others with much love and respect. As a result, I notice that when I travel with him, people always have fresh fruit, a nice piece of fish, fresh veggies, and a clean and healthy environment set up for him. Be good to you. People treat you how you treat yourself!

People seldom improve when they have no other model but themselves to copy. Who is your hero? Without heroes, we are all plain people who don't know how far we can go. The right role models can be very inspirational. As you get older it is harder to have heroes, but it is necessary, nonetheless.

Don't get sidetracked. Never let a change of job, a new environment, or a new partnership diminish your integrity. If you've been eating right, praying, and exercising for ten years, continue to do so. Have you been slipping? All it takes is a couple of days of saying "I will make it to the gym tomorrow" and before you know it, it's become "I will make it to the gym next week." Or, "Oh, its just one ice cream sundae," which easily becomes "I only gained five pounds" and then "Oh, I can easily lose these fifteen pounds." Here's a good one: "I will make it to church next Sunday or God understands!" Yeah, God understands, the gym understands, your health understands. You're slipping! Small changes in your habits can help you or ruin you. Don't get distracted. Stay focused!

Difficulties are meant to rouse you, not discourage you. The human spirit is meant to grow stronger by conflict. Adversity causes some men to break, others to break records. Let your test become a testimony. Invite adversity in. Always remember. . . . A wounded deer leaps the highest.

Only passions, great passions, can elevate the soul to great things. Nothing great in the world has been accomplished without passion. Work hard. People who never get carried away, should be!

Are you poor? Do you find you're never satisfied? The covetous man is always poor! The richest man is he whose pleasures are the cheapest. True affluence is to not need anything. 1 Thessalonians 5:18 says, "In every thing give thanks." Always remember: Contentment is worth much more than riches!

Be happy. Be free. The end of all suffering is acceptance. Take all of your concerns and give them to the Most High. After you've done all that *you* can do, give it to God!

True genius is the ability to make everything easy. Life is actually easy, but we as human beings make it hard. A stroll in the park, a laugh with some friends, a black dress, white pearls, a black suit and white tie. Simplicity, carried to an extreme, becomes elegance!

To become successful is very simple. The blueprint is written in the self-help section of every bookstore. There's nothing new under the sun. If you really want to become successful you must learn to follow instructions and do what's right! When one bases their life on principle, 99 percent of their decisions are already made.

Clear your mind of worry! Be thankful this morning. Look on the bright side of things and watch doors begin to open. Anxiety and worry are two thieves.

How do you remain joyful? Be quick to forgive! Joy is restored to your life when you learn how to forgive and forget, and the two virtues work together.

GOD IS LOVE

If we want joy, we must have a lack of concern for old offenses. You will feel joy when you forgive the reckless offenses of others. You will feel joy when you forgive someone seven times for the same offense. Sounds crazy, right? It might not make sense to you, but the principle works. If you want to walk in joy, you will have to walk in forgiveness. Unforgiving people are frustrated people. Be happy and forgive those who have offended today!

All great breakthroughs show up when you are at peace. Anxiety and worry will chase your blessings away. You have only two options in life. You can try to do everything yourself, or you can let God do it for you. If you are going to let God do it for you, you don't have to camp on top of it mentally all the time, trying to dissect and figure it out. Allowing God to have total control of our lives also has a positive effect on our health. Here's the key: Do your best and give God the rest.

Men do not attract that which they want, but that which they are. A person's soul attracts that which he is secretly harboring. What are you thinking about? Your thoughts are your prayers. Your ambition, not your worded prayer, is your true creed. Remember that your inner conversation becomes your outward manifestation.

Success has nothing to do with what you gain in life or accomplish for yourself. It's what you do for others. *Sharing* what you have is the key to joy.

Are you happy? Do you have an exciting goal? They who have no central purpose in their life easily fall prey to petty worries, fears, troubles, and self-pity. Find a goal and make this goal your supreme duty. Mark out a straight pathway to its achievement. Don't look to the left or right. Doubts and fears must be rigorously excluded in order to achieve your goal. And remember to find joy in the process. Here's the key: Conceive of a legitimate purpose in your heart and set out to accomplish it.

GOD IS LOVE

You will always gravitate toward your secret desires. God doesn't answer your worded prayer as much as he answers your innermost thoughts. The Bible says the secret to prayer is to believe that you will receive what you want. Here's the problem: Most people pray for one thing and expect another. Remember that when you pray you don't get what you pray for, **you** get what you expect!

The sooner you realize that you need God, the better off you are. All who have walked with God have viewed prayer as the main business of their lives. Even if no command to pray had existed, our very weakness would have suggested it. Here's the key to success: ASK FOR HELP.

GOD IS LOVE

Life is actually simple. Ask yourself the secret to your success. Listen to your answer and practice it. Don't let discipline become a problem! The secret of discipline is motivation. When a man is sufficiently motivated, discipline will take care of itself!

Learn to focus on your service and not on your reward. Your reward will always take care of itself if your service is good. Many people feel underpaid but the truth of the matter is that if you have good product/service you won't have enough room in your bank account for the money. Stop counting your money and start serving!

GOD IS LOVE

Your family should be run like a business. The father and mother should be partners in the corporation. The children should have the responsibility of upholding, representing, and carrying on the family business. Communication is imperative. There should be weekly family meetings and one common goal to always love and protect each other.

efine what really brings you happiness and joy. Take stock of where your real satisfaction and sources of nurturance and support lie. Never let others define your goals and happiness. If being super successful and driving a Benz turns you on . . . then good for you. If a walk in the park, a nice lunch, and peace of mind equals a successful day for you, then so be it. Define your true joy today.

Happiness consists in giving and in serving others. The greatest happiness in the world is to make others happy. Remember, you cannot light another's path with your torch without lighting your own.

What you can tolerate you cannot change! An angry man is an awakened man. Many people want to change this country, but things will never change until someone is angry enough to step forward and take charge! When channeled correctly, anger is a powerful agency for change. Whether it's in your school, city elections, or for the next president, VOTE.

In the long run, the pessimist may be right, but the optimist has a better time on the trip.

We can either tiptoe through life and hope that we get to death without being too badly bruised or we can live a full, complete life achieving our goals and realizing our wildest dreams. Go for it. Have fun. Get out there and get in the game.

Make God your partner. His success record is astounding. Give him some money, too. Become a giver. Tithing works. Prayer begins where human capacity ends. A day without prayer is a boast against God. Seven days without prayer makes one weak.

Happiness is the product of an effort to make someone else happy. Life becomes harder for us when we live for others, but it also becomes richer and more joy-filled. As Paramahansa Yogananda says, when you learn to live for others, they will live for you.

Become conscious of being whatever it is that you desire to be. Don't let anyone define you. Define yourself! The Bible says in Proverbs 23:7, as a man "thinketh in his heart, so is he." Who do you say you are? Now that, and that alone, is all that counts. Now stick to the script.

Happiness is the meaning and the purpose of life,
the whole aim and end of human existence.
—Aristotle

All I can say about life is "Oh God enjoy it!"
—Bob Newhart

We have a duty to be happy. Work on it. There is no duty so much underrated as the duty of being happy. Like swimming, riding, writing, or playing golf, happiness can be learned.

Live mindful of how brief your life is. "It feels just like yesterday" is a statement we all say very often. Think about friends, loved ones, family, and colleagues who have passed. Cherish your moments. Minutes are worth more than money. Spend them wisely. Many people take no care of money till they come to the end of it, and others do just the same with their time. Some are here for a good time, not a long time. Live in the present. Enjoy!

Fortune befriends the bold. Audacity has made kings. Bravery and faith bring both material and spiritual rewards. Take courage. Be brave. He who loses wealth loses much; he who loses a friend loses more; but he who loses his courage loses all.

We must always change, renew, rejuvenate ourselves; otherwise, we harden. You must learn day by day, year by year, to broaden your horizons. The more things you love, the more you enjoy. But remember, the real voyage of discovery consists not in seeking new landscapes but in having new vision. What do you see?

Just like exercise invigorates you and helps to get you going, remember to pray and give yourself a pep talk every morning. We need spiritual and mental exercises every morning to stir us into action. By talking to yourself every hour of the day, you can direct yourself to think thoughts of courage and happiness, thoughts of power and peace. These words are just as true today as they were eighteen centuries ago when Marcus Aurelius first wrote them in his book *Meditations*: "Our life is what our thoughts make it."

You will only have significant success with something that is an obsession. Also remember, you will never be promoted until you become overqualified for your present position. Be obsessed with success!

Learn to listen to others' points of view. If you combine the thoughts you have with the thoughts of others, you will come up with thoughts you've never had! I have found that the BIGGEST successes I've ever had were not my ideas but a synthesis of various ideas. What happens if you don't open your parachute when you jump? Be open. It could save your life.

Pressure is intensifying in the world to such an unbelievable degree that I believe we need God even to get in and out of the grocery store and to remain calm in these troubled days. People need a prayerful life. Someone might ask: "How can I learn to pray?" Here's the answer—"Praying is learned by praying."

In Proverbs 11:14, the Bible says, "In the multitude of counselors there is safety." Always remember, two heads are better than one. Seek out help. Avoid isolation. Going solo may find you going So Low.

Don't be afraid of failing! You must look failure dead in the eyes and tell failure, YOU HAVE NO POWER OVER ME! You have to be able to look at failure the way the Master Jesus looked at death and said, "Oh, death where is thy sting?" Now get up, stay thankful, and smile and perform your miracle. Concentrating on a so-called failure is a waste of mind energy. Think on good things. Keep good thoughts and past victories in front of your mind's eye.

GOD IS LOVE

Do you ever feel rejected or not accepted by others? If your answer is yes, then remember this: How we feel about ourselves is a determining factor in our success in life and in relationships. When we reject ourselves, it may seem to us that others reject us as well. People see you as you see yourself. When you start feeling good about you, others will, too!

Are you your biggest fan? In order to make it in life, we must root for ourselves. Make sure you are your own cheerleader. Look at yourself in the mirror and say, "I am great." Self-love is a cornerstone of success. Once you do that, things begin to change.

We must use the eyes behind the eyes constantly. Never let what you see with your physical eyes become more real to you than what you see with your spiritual eyes. Stay creative, use your imagination, change constantly. Go to new places, see new people, change where you eat, where you travel, the kinds of books you read. Like hip-hop? Check out the opera. Fan of mysteries? Try some history. Don't get stuck in a rut. There's a big world out there. Make a new move today.

Don't be afraid to ask. Asking is proof that you've conquered pride. In most cases asking causes us to become humble. Don't be afraid to keep asking. Just because someone turns you down on a date the first time doesn't mean that they are going to say no the next time. You didn't get into the program you're interested in? Reapply. Asking keeps you humble. And that's what God wants.

What you know determines how far you go. Your success will be determined by your knowledge. What do you know? Who do you hang with? Get people around you who know something. The Bible says we perish for lack of knowledge. People that understand great landscaping will have greener grass. You are either strengthened or limited by your knowledge. GET IN THE KNOW.

Don't take life so seriously. Life is a game. Play to win. If you lose one day, there's always tomorrow. When problems arise, try to figure it out but don't complain. Get out there and work hard, have fun, and relax. It always works out in the end.

GOD IS LOVE

If you want something you've never had, you have to do something you've never done before. Do something new. Challenge yourself.

Learn to take responsibility for everything that happens in your life. The problem with many people is that they think circumstances or people can block their blessings. But your blessings start and end with you. Say these words every day and begin to free yourself: No one is doing anything to me but me.

Happy is he who learns how to bear
what he cannot change!
—J. C. F. von Schiller

Seek not happiness too greedily,
and be not fearful of unhappiness.
—Lao-tzu

Don't be upset with life's ups and downs. Don't call life unfair. Don't focus or complain about past hurts and pains. Learn to forgive and forget. The end of all suffering is acceptance.

Success is going from failure to failure without losing enthusiasm. A person can succeed at almost anything for which he has unlimited enthusiasm. The world belongs to the energetic!

We don't understand everything that God is doing, nor do we need to. The Bible says that all things work together for good. All of your hurts and pains. All of your disappointments and hang-ups are for God's Glory! They are your teachers. It seems incomprehensible that Nelson Mandela would be imprisoned for so long, but once free he was elected president of South Africa. In the rap field, Kanye West's painful car accident led to an influential and successful album. 50 Cent was shot nine times, yet from his pain came his superstardom. Coincidence? I doubt it. Just rest and know that Father knows best. Jesus died on the cross just to be resurrected three days later. He was hung up for your hang-ups! Your pain is gain. Let God have his way.

GOD IS LOVE

To expect life to be tailored to our specifications is to invite frustration. Too many people miss the silver lining because they're expecting gold. Slow down, breathe. Learn to enjoy the little things; there are so many of them.

We always have enough to be happy about if we are enjoying that which we do have—and not worrying about that which we don't. Only man destroys what is, with thoughts of what may be. A man who is about to be sent to jail or is on his deathbed always thinks, What a wonderful life I've had. I only wish I'd realized it sooner. No one succeeds without effort. Those who succeed owe their success to their perseverance. Big shots are only little shots who keep shooting!

Any idiot can face a crisis—it's day-to-day living that wears you out. Peace hath higher tests of manhood than battle ever knew.

GOD IS LOVE

There are three types of baseball players—those who make it happen, those who watch it happen, and those who wonder what happened.

—Tommy Lasorda

Your future depends on many things, but mostly on you. The best place to find a helping hand is at the end of your own arm!

The happy person knows his or her possibilities and limitations! No one knows *you* better than you. If people want you to do things, use your imagination to foresee how these things will look in the end. If the final result doesn't fit your personality or strengths, don't do it. Always set yourself up to win. 99.9 percent of the time, if I can't see the victory, I don't do it. My answer is, "No! Hell no, I ain't doing that!" Know thyself!

Do the work, but trust in God. The person who has a firm trust in the Most High is powerful by His power, wise by His wisdom, happy by His happiness.

The difference between the rich and the poor is that the rich are decisive. Life is just a series of questions that require a decision, a direction. Life is the sum of all your choices. Here's the bottom line: When one bases his life on principle, 99 percent of his decisions are already made.

Have you taken a good look at yourself? Before you go to bed every night go over your day and look at your actions. Are you patient, kind, giving? Do yourself a favor and take a good look at your life. Are your actions well thought out or are they wild? As Socrates said, "The unexamined life is not worth living." It's examination time. Examine your life today!

Having a family is a great pleasure. Protect your family life with diligence. Remember, the thief only shows up at a loaded vault.

There are two thieves in your life! These two thieves are trying to rob you! Don't get jacked of your peace. Don't get robbed of your fun. Don't let worry beat you down. These two thieves are the past and the future! The past is history, the future is a mystery, the present is a gift, and that's why we call it the present. It's a gift! Seize the day.

Learn to forgive people. When you don't forgive people you are actually holding on to emotions that can cripple you. Being unforgiving hurts you more than it hurts the unforgiven! When you don't forgive you block your blessings. God forgives us every time. People make mistakes. Forgive everyone today. Be the bigger person. The philosopher Alexander Pope said, "To err is human, to forgive, divine."

Worry often gives a small thing a big shadow. Stop worrying. Worry doesn't help tomorrow's troubles, but it does ruin today's happiness.

Do you have a plan for success? Show me what you're working with. A strategy that doesn't take into account resources is doomed to failure. Take an inventory. How much time do you have? What kinds of materials, supplies, or inventory do you have? Take quiet time to think! Strategic thinking is like cleansing yourself. You have to time and again.

The number one enemy that a man has is himself. Don't beat yourself up so much. You will make mistakes. The only man who makes no mistakes is the man who never does anything. Enjoy life. Forgive yourself. Here's what actress Rosalind Russell said: "Flops are a part of life's menu, and I've never been a girl to miss out on any of the courses!"

Many people check the scale weekly hoping for weight loss, but do very little to change their diet. Many people go to church every week and hope that God will help them, but never follow any instructions from the priest. You gotta do something. Do something you've never done to get something you've never had. I often say, "Sitting in a church won't make a person a Christian any more than sitting in a garage will make them a car."

*The human spirit is stronger
than anything that can happen to it.*
—George C. Scott

*Sorrow is a fruit. God does not allow
it to grow on a branch that is too weak to bear it.
The will of God will not take you
where the grace of God cannot keep you.*
—Anonymous

Trouble creates a capacity to handle it.
—Oliver Wendell Holmes, Jr.

Start your week off on the right foot. Learn to be at peace. Relax. Your ability to harmonize with the universe brings blessings. If you don't have money it could be a sign that you're not walking in harmony. You must be in harmony to have money. Your inner conflict will push blessings away. Get rid of anxiety, become thankful, and watch the blessings pour in.

Don't be timid when you pray; rather, batter the very
gates of heaven with storms of prayer.
—Anonymous

We may as well not pray at all as offer
our prayers in a lifeless manner.
—William S. Plumer

God never denied that soul anything that
traveled as far as heaven to ask for it.
—John Trapp

The effectual fervent prayer
of a righteous man availeth much.
—James 5:16

GOD IS LOVE

Happiness is action, to fill the hour, and leave no crevice. That is happiness. Happiness is often the result of being too busy to be miserable. Those that are happy usually find joy in the fierce and ruthless battles of life. The most exquisite pleasure is giving pleasure to others.

Never value materiality over spirituality. That's why in Mark 10:21, Jesus told the rich young ruler to go sell everything and give it to the poor. He didn't mean give all of your possessions and money to poor people. God meant feed your poor spirit! Get into spirituality! Put your belief system on display. The Lord was saying you've given more attention to things than to the King. God wants You in His camp. Remember, it's okay to have things, but never let things have you!

GOD IS LOVE

Prayer honors God, acknowledges His being, exalts His power, adores His providence, secures His aid. What do you need? Ask for it. You can like it or not, but asking is the rule of the Kingdom! God's ear lies close to the believer's lip!

God gives us strength enough, and sense enough
for everything He wants us to do.
—John Ruskin

Courage mounteth with occasion.
—William Shakespeare

Be at peace! Are you doing your best? Do your best and forget the rest. That's the will of God! One mystic said, "Everyone is doing the best they can!" Everyone. That's right, EVERYONE! Even the guy who keeps going to jail over and over. If people knew a better way to do things and be happy they would do it! Don't be so hard on yourself or on other people. Remember, everyone is doing the best they can! Have a good day! Smile! Laugh! Do your best and forget the rest!

Progress always involves risk. In baseball, you can't steal second base and keep your foot on first! When the press asked one great player why he didn't choke up and swing for average, he screamed, "Cadillacs are down at the end of the bat!" He then pulled off in his new car. Always remember this: "Only those who dare to fail greatly can ever achieve greatly." —Robert F. Kennedy

GOD IS LOVE

What fascinates you? What draws you in? What you are fascinated with becomes fastened to you! What gets your attention? Horror movies? Car accidents? Be careful, fascination has power. Become fascinated with good health, wealth, beauty, or luxury. Remember, whatever you think about and look at you become! Have a fascinating day.

Isolation is sickness. Give your burdens to God. Pray often! Ask others for help! Life is much easier when we stick together. Always remember this: One snowflake is frail, but when snow sticks together it can stop traffic. Isolation leads to failure.

Destruction precedes renewal. If you don't pierce an abscess with a knife, how can it heal and how can you regain your health? When a tailor cuts up cloth piece by piece, does anyone go up to him and ask, "Why have you torn up this beautiful satin?" Just count all of your troubles as joy! If you don't subject wheat to the grinding millstone, how will bread ever come to decorate your table? Don't worry. Count all of your pain as joy!

GOD IS LOVE

Make up your mind. Quickly. Hurry! Often the greatest risks are involved in postponement rather than in making a wrong decision. Do not wait for ideal circumstances or the best opportunities; they will never come. Remember this. "Deliberation often loses a good chance." —Latin proverb

What are you passionate about? What would you do every day even if you weren't paid for it? Answer that question . . . tell the truth. Life will pay you wages for your service. Don't focus on money more than you focus on service. Find your passion and you'll find your money. Do what you love and the money will follow.

Learn something new as often as you can. I find that I earn more money in this stage of my life, now that I have come and sat at the feet of Masters.

If we wait to do something until we are not afraid, we will probably accomplish very little. Here's the key to accomplishing something big when you're afraid to do it. Do it even though you are afraid! Be determined that your life is not going to be ruled by fear. One scary day, many years ago, fear came knocking at my door and when faith answered for me, no one was there. WHEN FAITH SHOWS UP, FEAR DISAPPEARS!

GOD IS LOVE

NOTES

NOTES

NOTES

NOTES